Journey of Trees

poems by
Susan Landgraf

A Publication of The Poetry Box®

Poems © 2024 Susan Landgraf
All rights reserved.

Editing & Book Design by Shawn Aveningo Sanders
Cover Image licensed via Envato
Cover Design by Shawn Aveningo Sanders

No part of this book may be republished without permission from the author, except in the case of brief quotations embodied in critical essays, epigraphs, reviews and articles, or publisher/author's marketing collateral.

Finalist in The Poetry Box Chapbook Prize 2023
ISBN: 978-1-956285-58-1
Published in the United States of America
Wholesale Distribution by Ingram Group

Published by The Poetry Box®, May 2024
Portland, Oregon, United Sates
website: ThePoetryBox.com

*This book is for all the women in my life
who have given me fortitude, blessings, love and words.*

*This book is for all the men in my life
who have given me the same.*

I, like trees, have learned to adapt and thrive.

Contents

Apple	9
Starting the Fire	11
Old Is This Road and Foxes	12
Time	13
Childhood Tree	14
Waiting for the Prince	15
Preserving	16
Cedar Talk	17
The Wise Know Nothing At All Well Maybe One Song	18
Finding the Bones	19
On the Branch of a Chestnut Tree	20
Suite of Sycamores	21
Woman Who Plants the First Glory Cedar	23
Orchard after the Harvest	24
Remember	25
Second Birthing Hut	26
Crows in Conversation among the Hemlocks	27
Tower Window	28
The Difference	29
The Ten Stations of Worship	30
Nodes	31
The Apple	32
Choosing the Gardener	33
Daffodils	34
Fallen Cypress	35
Winter Apples	36
Psalm Tree	37

Game Board with Broom	38
Under the Babylonian Willow	39
Last Stop	40
Exodus	41
Acknowledgments	43
About the Author	45

We lose our trees.
We lose our birds.
We lose our myths.

—*Anonymous*

Apple

    1.

There she was minding her own business
no clothes to fold
                      Adam off somewhere
when she questioned
     why the deer could eat the fallen fruit
     but she was forbidden.

When who should appear?

No garden proposition has been as dramatic since.

    2.

One bite and she was left
with vaginal infections and fallen arches.

She could forgive Adam his fear
                   not his blame.

    3.

They carried names
out of Eurasia   Orange Pippin, Sheepnose,
                      Grimes Golden, Gala

their white blossoms falling like snow
over the thorny rose.
               She learned to cut
their stems without pricking her finger.
                Learned not to fear blood

and to graft apple trees for the best harvest.

[. . .]

4.

She told her daughters
and they told their daughters
> *how tart*
> *how sweet.*

Starting the Fire

Kneeling
she remembered white forks
flicking the trees
lighting them to char.

She had to climb, leap quick
into the pyramid of mosses
and twigs. She knew
she would not crawl out of the ash.

She would not be able to prove
she invented fire.

Old Is This Road and Foxes

The white fox hat covers more
than her ears and neck. Eyes
hold memories, and she walks
that field of hemp in even rows,
a road so narrow
down the page, its lament
lasts this long:

>The 12th century Ch'i, on her way
>to be wed, saw a sly fox tread.
>She asked the fox, *Who gave permission
>to give me to a man?*
>
>A baby bird with the scent
>of human fingers
>on her breast, she would be kept
>behind her husband's gate.
>
>*Flee into the woods fast,
>faster,* the fox cried.
>But even the fire-star
>could lead no rescue.

She turns, thanks the fox.
Luna breaks over the pines, and she
is a winter firefly
through the woods. She knows
this direction,
>this darkness,
>this fur.

Time

       runs blind.

Buddha sits under the boojum tree.

Mimir guards a sacred spring at the root of the World Tree.

Ganesh holds his sword of mango wood.

Freyja comes on Christmas and shakes the apple trees for a good harvest.

Christ carries his ironwood cross.

Muhammed goes dawn to desert, dusk to death

       and time runs in the forests, oasis, mountains—

    this mystery
of myrtle wood and baobab
    rhythm
of aspen, hawthorn, birch

      and bristlecone pines

that know
how to live
four-thousand years.

Childhood Tree

In sieved moonlight
wood splinters pricked her feet

Its smoothed hollow
held her

First star
she wished a nest of flannel arms

She waited for the call home
to supper

The star hung speared
on a leafless branch

Waiting for the Prince

Pricked her finger on a hickory spindle.
Flowered every twenty-eight days

knowing like the dogwood that what passes for petals
aren't.

Knowing the real blossoms cluster,
inconspicuous.

Tired of sorrowful men crying
in their hollow-bottomed cups,

she went to the sea where it all began,
the prince crying *come back, come back*

lost
in the sound of the ocean's waves.

She knew she would come to herself
full again.

Preserving

Like a low-throated train
sea fills the air.

Sand and cedars
testify to place.

Salt grass scratches her cheek
and she tastes blood,

the gypsy singing her veins,
spring cracking open the salt air.

Standing the course
like a two-limbed tree,

she believes in the bud.
She believes in the brine.

Cedar Talk

She listens to the waves that never die
        and the wind talks
        to knife-sharp grasses
that can cut an eye.
        Wind talks with the Quinault
        where it empties into the sea, scours
the clapboard siding, turns a dog's tail
        between its legs. Wind carries seagulls
        shrieking to the fish house roof, shakes
the blue and white tsunami signs.
        At the headwaters where Chinook
        and Hoh, Queets and Quileute meet,
raven's wings shadow the mercantile,
        raven who brought light
        to the Canoe and Cedar people.
This is where salmon ran so thick people
        walked on water. Here the cedars
        have joined their roots underground.
Nugguam means to "talk"
        and this is their truth
        in their talk with the wind.

THE WISE KNOW NOTHING AT ALL WELL MAYBE ONE SONG
—Ikkyu

The moon again scythes the darkness.
A flute plays the birches.
One pool and all the demons come out to drink.

The moon again scythes the darkness.
Tigers crouch in the closet. Snakes coil under the bed.
The candle burns. A moth's wings singe.

The moon scythes the darkness again.
Under the red blanket she's a curled ridge.
Her eyelashes whisper a star-dark field.

Finding the Bones

Among the maple leaves
        and grasses
                she got down on her knees.
                      She found bird skeletons

in the blackberry tangles
        and the laughter
                of berry-stained children
                      who had shinnied apple trees

before they knew about gallows
        and witch burnings, about Eve and Adam,
                before they diagrammed
                      their genealogical limbs.

On the Branch of a Chestnut Tree

She can't see the whole tree but through the barred window she talks to the blossoms. She calls them children. *So many children.* The sun is covered with ash.

She traces the knobby branch on the glass. Talks to her husband who smelled of tobacco and wool. He surprised her with peppermint candies. There were no children.

She fingers the blossoms, her apron heavy with plums, purple, and the sweet juice runs down her chin. The air clots. She calls the blossoms children. She croons a song her father taught: *...Dai, da-ye-nu, Dai, da-ye-nu...*, watches men dig up the graves.

She taps the branch through the barred window, calls the blossoms traitors. Wipes the rain drops off the glass with her sleeve.

Suite of Sycamores

Wind like a dragon's tail shakes
the six trees with their three-lobed leaves,
a crow's nest anchored in the tallest. Spiked
spherical fruit swings from the branches.
Shadows lengthen. The fledgling calls
more insistent.

Sparrow song swirls the August afternoons
until dragon fire scorches the lawns.
A singer's voice etched in #13 plastic
never wavers: Surely if God watches over
lilies, sparrows—and chickadees, bushtits,
towhees... The fledgling quiets.

Students study differences: ravens larger,
crows stout-bodied, both omnivorous.
Poe wrote: *Shadowy, shadowy...*
How it hangs upon the trees,/ A mystery of mysteries!
The *Baltimore Clipper* reported
Poe died of "congestion of the brain."

Autumn's end, songbirds migrate.
Crows stay strung on the phone lines.
The air rusts. Parachuting scales
and fruit with wing-like seeds
with their roots in the Nile
shirrrrrr a litany of foreclosure.

By December the six trees skeleton
a grey sky choked with fog and rain.
Once nothing had a name—
not river, tree, February, time—only
sound and shadows. Small branches
fall like discarded antlers.

Crow caw, like an aulos,
cuts the wind. In the battle
between Apollo and dragons,
the double-seeded sycamores
are pipes playing the march
of the wooden soldiers.

Woman Who Plants the First Glory Cedars

She believes in healing stones that fit in her palm,
speaking to her lifelines, and the power of psalms.

She dreams of finding sea-smoothed bottle glass
from a sea she's never seen. Knows that her past

lives hold the tides in her blood, obeying the moon.
Her country is forged of clay, no turtles or loons.

Back-yard smoke rises up some days so hot it burns
holes in the clouds, but there is no rain. Her skin itches

for water. The people, their throats dried-up river beds,
beg for water. They beseech gods who have gone deaf.

She goes years back to her mother's soft voice and a myth.
That night she dances, crying, on the drum skin of the earth.

After three days, rain. She hears waves crash, feels the pull
of tides. Knows the glory cedars will serve her people.

Orchard after the Harvest

    1.

Her son remembered the lesson
of the Little Red Hen, but this was
an orchard with only a ditch to cross.

He raised his arms
for the apple, the world framed
in a green-tinted sky.

    2.

Winter with its wizened fruit
and leggy wrinkled potatoes
waited. Under a stack of papers

her son had left behind,
she found the photograph
she'd snapped of him
                      reaching.

Remember

blossoms drifting like pink snow
women knowing
stirrings in the heart
and secret places
moist with minds of their own
this taste
for a Golden Delicious

Second Birthing Hut

Tree fallen like a giant bleached umbilical cord
and a dozen logs—inside that house
of mismatched bones, the sound of the sea came in.

Inside that house of mismatched bones facing sea
and sky, nothing still—clouds, eagles, gulls,
her steepled fingers learning the lay of his body.

His body edging closer to death, he listened
to the sea and her fingers, let guilt go
inside that house of bones facing west and sky.

Crows in Conversation among the Hemlocks

A dead gull is anchored among the wrack
in the sand, neck crooked west. Six gulls keep
their distance. They do not speak.

A crow lands on the gull, cocks his head
left, caws right. Another crow answers.
The dead gull's eyes stay fixed.

The crow pecks and tugs at the entrails
the color of shore foam. Beak in,
then his head, he pulls and swallows.

Some distance away, gulls keep their vigil.
More crows join in and carry on
their conversation until

the sea resurrects the dead,
whose kind have now turned
their backs to the wind.

Tower Window

~after Clayton James' ceramic "Untitled"

She doesn't have hair like Rapunzel's.
There is no door.
No prince in the woods.

Five pomegranates fall
in the rain. Or maybe ropes
of lightning she can't climb.

The landscape in this story
has no blackberry mazes
or brambles. No firs or hemlocks.

In the tower's back
a bear paw. After
the forest fire

she settles in.
Smoke holds
the sun for ransom.

The Difference

River knows the sea
by leaving, and trees
                      stand naked
along its banks for the winter run.

Between bark and heart, rings
hold the years
                before woodcutters
chose to make a table, a coffin or bed.

On the shortest day, she runs
her fingers over the cold bark
                        searching for
the promise—buds swelling

in spite of forest fires, floods,
and droughts.
              Between
fire and memory the river.

The Ten Stations of Worship

This is the hand held for safety's sake,
palms raised to show the most traveled paths.

This is the foot, bunioned and mud-stained—Russian
steppes, ice caves, olive groves.

This is the leg, striding or curved, lotus-like
in the California poppies.

This is the eye of curled ferns and symbols.
This is the eye of permission. Amen.

This is the lap, a nest of goose down.
We've learned to fold and to wait.

This is the breast we come to and come to—
our need for suckle and beauty and grace.

This is the seed pod moist
with rain.

This is the other mouth
we depend on—the telling and retelling

in this temple of trees.

Nodes

They ascend
branch
arc
intersect
hold

They curve
ecliptic
symbiotic
periodic
astronomic

They speak
vertex
rheumatic
diversify
stay

They cross
boundaries
fences
sewer lines
They midwife

in silence
Bamboo
Potatoes
Whisk Ferns
Grasses

The Apple

Possibly you know Welty's "...Visit of Charity:"
two old women and how they lived,
their nursing home like a robber's cave;
and the Campfire girl, her apple hid under
a bush, her innocence the cost of doing good.

Possibly you know women mostly
are left to mourning and nursing
homes, leftovers in a world of urine
and silence, whatever they knew of poetry
and tenderness spit up or soured.

Possibly you're asking: Where's that
Campfire girl? Why hasn't she opened
a window to let in the scent of lilacs?
Why isn't she sharing that delicious apple,
that little light under a bushel?

Perhaps you've read Gallagher,
who believes Saint Teresa's
Words lead to deeds, who gave
Ray Carver a room in her house,
a room in the house that poetry built.

Possibly you've heard Carver is dead.
But that night at Elliott Bay, his one lung gone,
the other failing, the audience applauded;
people laughed and wept until he wasn't wheezing.
Saint Teresa also said that words *...prepare the soul.*

Choosing the Gardener

She would choose the way
he puts thumb and fingers around
handles, his patience turning
the soil for tulips in April.

She would choose the soft
hollows his knees make
in the soil, a man who
doesn't apologize for worship
or touch.

She would choose him to teach
her naming and differences:
crab apple from plum, supple
birches from peeling madrones.

Oh, gardener, she would say, speak
to me of mulch, of barrows
and beds. Tell me how you
order daily what the ground
bulges and buckles.

She would choose, yes,
a gardener who keeps his tools clean
and sharp, oh, a gardener
who isn't afraid to cut.

Daffodils

Through winter and her children
who cut and ran

it would be easy to whimper,
to give in to dry rot.

The fences she and her husband built
have fallen in the wind and snow.

What resurrection she gets
comes from a bulb

whose bloom will be dead in a week.
But she looks for

these harbingers of spring waving
around the fence posts,

their petals brushing
the slivered wood.

Fallen Cypress

She has gone to sit with its death,
this tree an offspring of the branch
that Zardusht brought back from Paradise
and planted before the gate of Kashmar.

She wipes the droplets like tears
from its trunk, talks about its history
of mummy cases, holders of the ashes
of the battle dead. *You are a symbol*

of fullness, youth, and freedom in Iran.
You mean joy and grace in the Himalayas.
You're the plantation that's thought to be
sufficient for any young woman's marriage.

She fills her cupped hands with the sea
and sprinkles the cypress.
You're the first tree that I'll see
in the underworld.

Winter Apples

August branches droop
their crop

like a ballerina's arms
at the end

of practice.
Globes glow

in October's changing
light. Some spotted.

Some wormed.
Most fell.

The rest froze
on their limbs,

chartreuse December
stillborns.

Birds peck
the liquor-rich spheres.

The branches
dance.

Psalm Tree

Dearest willow, which art in weeping,
sorrow hath begotten your name.
You reach out of the blood-soaked ground
to be baptized by the rain.

Shelter these women from howling winds,
keep their secrets while they weave baskets
to carry across the desert and mountains.

And when they reach the other side, give
them relief from their aches and pains,

give them, willow-father, wisdom and your branches
to ward the evil spirits off.

Game Board with Broom

Perched without wings, her toe tips
the white-wire trees.

    Before leaves,
they patterned black and white tiles
to look like cracks, the painted walls
blue as jays.

    Imagine air that shades
days without fear. Picture the moves
a hand with nimble fingers makes,
the moods a dancer executes.

    The season has cut its losses,
the ballet its troupe. Her three
feathers' worth of chances
flutter. She's thinking resolve.

She's humming a rescuer's sweet talk
while she sweeps up the pieces.

Under the Babylonian Willow

Trees in her life had not been personal
until her father cut a branch and she became
the Babylonian wearing the willow.
He knows not what he does, the priest intoned. *Do not blame.*

She grew afraid of forgiveness. She found
libraries where she discovered deciduous—
that state of shedding and wait—daughter cells and
cambium layers, heartwood. She learned how trees hush

around strangers, wedge cracks in the sidewalk.
Felled by the wind, they grow into nurse logs.
They dance on one leg, their crowns brushing sky—hawks,
robins, crows in their branches in full sun or fog.

On hillsides, in valleys—Ginkgo. Hazelnut. Pine. Aspen.
She watched for nimbuses. She prayed for baptism.

Last Stop

She'd bound
her husband's wounds, done his laundry,
fed his hunger with food
and compliance.

She'd tended the four children out of six
who took root—watered and fertilized
with praise until they bloomed:
Antonio, Violet, Rosemary, Ren—

and watched the eight-ten train
whistling daily past her door.

She knows each flower bed and garden
with her knees and nose.

The willow she planted fifty years
ago moans like a hundred reed whistles.
She sings lullabies, and the weeping
branches hold her.

Next month when the freeway
is laid through her tree,
she will climb.

Exodus

~after a drawing titled "Ancient" by Gillian Griffiths

The massive turtle carrying pine trees
on its back looks like something ripped
out of a geological past: clawed toes,
dragon-like tail, massive thighs.
You can tell it's an old soul under
a thin membrane of light in the sky
with some birds. It's a slow exodus.
Maybe the last forest, maybe the last
birds, maybe this last turtle holding steady
in a pattern of lines, curves, crevasses
and peaks inching forward with its burden
of hope. A pinprick of light, yes,
in a shrouded world where a few birds
find trees they can build their nests in.

Acknowledgments

With gratitude to the editors of the journals who published the following poems, some revised and with different titles:

Calyx: "Old Is This Road and Foxes"

Empty Bowl: "Cedar Talk"

Museum of Modern Art website: "Tower Window"

Persimmon Tree: "Under the Babylonian Willow"

Pontoon: "The Difference"

Sabella: "Orchard"

About the Author

Susan Landgraf received an Academy of American Poet Laureates grant, resulting in *A Muckleshoot Poetry Anthology: At the Confluence of the Green and White Rivers*, which she curated; Washington State University Press published it in early 2024. Her other books include *Crossings* (Ravenna Press), *The Inspired Poet* (Two Sylvias Press), *What We Bury Changes the Ground* (Tebot Bach), and *Other Voices*. More than 400 poems have appeared in *Nimrod, Prairie Schooner, Poet Lore, Third Wednesday,* and others.

Landgraf served as Auburn's Poet Laureate from 2018-2020. She has given more than 150 workshops in the US and abroad and is the recipient of a Theodore Morrison Scholar Poetry Award for Breadloaf and Artist Trust, Jack Straw, and King County Arts Commission grants. A former journalist, she taught at Highline College for 30 years and at Shanghai Jiao Tong University. She loves epiphanies and believes poetry can save you.

About The Poetry Box®

The Poetry Box, a boutique publishing company in Portland, Oregon, provides a platform for both established and emerging poets to share their words with the world through beautiful printed books and chapbooks.

Feel free to visit the online bookstore (thePoetryBox.com), where you'll find more titles including:

gOD: A Respectfully Divergent Testament
by Penelope Scambly Schott

Reading Wind by Carol Barrett

When All Else Fails by Lana Hechtman Ayers

Earthwork by Kristin Berger

The Squannacook at Dawn by Richard Jordan

A Nest in the Heart by Vivienne Popperl

This Is the Lightness by Rachel Barton

Inside Out by Kirsten Morgan

Self Dissection by Amelia Diaz Ettinger

The Further Adventures of Zen Patriach Dōgen
by James K. Zimmerman

Kansas Reimagined by Anara Guard

Remote Control by Laura Esther Sciortino

Lighting Up the Duff by Sheila Sondik

Now Is What Matters by Janet Steward

Jump Straight Up by Jarold Ramsey

and more . . .

www.ingramcontent.com/pod-product-compliance
Lightning Source LLC
LaVergne TN
LVHW050030080526
838202LV00070B/6988